BOB KNIGHT

Life Beyond the Court: Bob Knight's   Post-Coaching
Journey

Michal E. Erickson

TABLE OF CONTENT

INTRODUCTION

Bob Knight, a name that resounds all through the ball world, is a famous figure in the game's set of experiences. Known for his extreme energy, steady obligation to greatness, and a training style that was both worshiped and scolded, Sway Knight's effect on the sport of ball is incomprehensible. This presentation makes way for a profound jump into the life and profession of a man whose impact arrived a long way past the ball court.

Brought into the world on October 25, 1940, in Massillon, Ohio, Weave Knight's excursion through the universe of balls is one of amazing ups and testing downs. As a player, he made progress at the university level, and as a mentor, he turned into an incredible figure, especially during his time at Indiana College. With a celebrated profession that has traversed many years

In any case, Bounce Knight was something beyond a b-ball mentor. His persona, portrayed by blazing eruptions and a tireless quest for flawlessness, made him a polarizing figure. This book intends to investigate the diverse existence of Weave Knight, from his initial days on the court to his change into broadcasting and the perseverance through inheritance he abandoned.

In the accompanying sections, we will dig into his training reasoning, his effect on players, the contentions that frequently encircled him, and the enduring impact he had on the sport of ball. We will likewise investigate the man behind the mentor, his own life, and the intricacies that characterized his personality.

Weave Knight's story is one of victory and unrest, enthusiasm and discipline, triumphs and discussions. His story is one that can't be told in simple measurements or titles; it requires a more profound investigation to genuinely comprehend the man behind the legend. Thus, we should leave on this excursion to reveal the striking life and profession of Sway Knight, a ball symbol like no other.

CHAPTER 1, WHO IS BOB KNIGHT

Bob Knight, whose complete name is Robert Montgomery Knight, is a previous American b-ball mentor and quite possibly one of the most unmistakable and disputable figures throughout the entire existence of school ball. He was brought into the world on October 25, 1940, in Massillon, Ohio.

Knight is most popular for his effective training profession, especially during his experience as the lead trainer of the Indiana College Hoosiers from 1971 to 2000. Under his administration, the Hoosiers made huge progress, including three NCAA public titles (in 1976, 1981, and 1987) and various meeting titles.

Knight was eminent for his training reasoning, which underscored areas of strength for an ethic, restrained play, and a guarantee of protection. He was many times portrayed by his extraordinary and, in some cases, fierce training style, which remembered important eruptions for the sidelines.

Notwithstanding, his vocation was likewise set apart by discussions and episodes. Knight's unstable attitude and activities prompted various disciplinary issues and eventually his expulsion from Indiana College in 2000.

Subsequent to leaving Indiana, Knight kept on instructing at Texas Tech College from 2001 to 2008, before resigning from training. He likewise filled in as a TV baseball observer.

Bounce Knight's heritage in the realm of balls is perplexing. While he is commended for his instructing accomplishments and his effect on the game, he remains a polarizing figure because of his dubious way of behaving and fierce training style. His impact on the game and his players, as well as his commitments to training reasoning, are subjects of both adoration and analysis.

1:1 SWAY KNIGHT IMPORTANCE IN THE REALM OF BALL

Sway Knight's importance in the realm of ball is multi-layered and lastingly affects the game. Here are a few critical parts of his importance:

Training Achievement: Sway Knight is prestigious for his training accomplishments, especially during his residency at Indiana College. He drove the Indiana Hoosiers to three NCAA public titles (in 1976, 1981, and 1987), displaying his capacity to fabricate winning groups. His obligation to guard and train was an exclusive requirement for progress in school ball.

Training Theory: Knight's training reasoning, underlining difficult work, readiness, and thoughtfulness regarding essentials have affected the game. A large number his instructing standards keep on being educated and carried out by mentors at all degrees of b-ball.

Player Advancement: Knight assumed a critical role in fostering the abilities and character of his players. Various competitors who played under his tutelage had fruitful vocations in the NBA, and then some. His training techniques were instrumental in molding the vocations of numerous expert baseball players.

Debate and Energy: Knight's blazing and fierce instructing style, combined with his serious enthusiasm for the game, made him an attractive figure. He was known for his profound eruptions uninvolved and his constant quest for flawlessness, which made the two admirers and pundits

Influence on Instructing and Initiative: Past b-ball, Sway Knight's authority style and standards have been contemplated and adjusted in different fields, including business and executives. His obligation to teach and his solid administration characteristics keep on moving forerunners in various areas.

Broadcast and Editorial: In the wake of resigning from training, Sway Knight changed into broadcasting and gave smart analysis on the ball. His experiences and skills enhanced the inclusion of the game, further cementing his presence in the baseball world.

Mentorship and Training: Knight's commitments to schooling and mentorship are, in many cases, eclipsed by his training vocation and contentions. He made huge gifts to colleges and upheld instructive drives, making an imprint past the ball court.

In synopsis, Sway Knight's importance in the realm of b-ball lies in his training achievement, compelling training reasoning, player improvement, and his effect on the more extensive domains of authority and schooling. His inheritance, while set apart by the two victories and discussions, remains a fundamental piece of the historical backdrop of the game.

CHAPTER 2, EARLY LIFE

Bob Knight, born on October 25, 1940, in Massillon, Ohio, had a humble and relatively unremarkable early life that laid the foundation for his later success in the world of basketball. Here are some key points about his early life:

Family Background: Bob Knight was the son of Hazel and Clevenger Knight. He grew up in a working-class family in Ohio. His father worked as a welder, and his mother was a homemaker.

High School Basketball: Knight attended Orrville High School in Orrville, Ohio. He played basketball for the school and was a standout player. His passion for the game began to develop during his high school years.

Academic and Athletic Excellence: Knight was not only a talented basketball player but also an excellent student. He graduated as class valedictorian in 1958.

College Playing Career: After high school, Knight continued his basketball career at Ohio State University. He played as a reserve on the Ohio State Buckeyes team and was a part of the squad that won the national championship in 1960.

Military Service: Following his college career, Bob Knight served in the United States Army. During his service, he began his coaching career as an assistant coach for the Army Black Knights' basketball team, which marked the start of his coaching journey.

Early Coaching Experiences: Knight's early coaching experiences at Army and as a high school coach in Cuyahoga Falls, Ohio, helped him develop his coaching style and philosophy.

These early life experiences, including his upbringing, high school basketball, and college playing career, laid the groundwork for Bob Knight's future success in coaching. His time in the military and early coaching roles provided him with valuable experience and knowledge that he would later apply in his coaching career at the collegiate level.

2:1 PLAYING CAREER

Bob Knight had a notable college playing career as a member of the Ohio State Buckeyes basketball team. Here are some key details about his playing career:

College Career at Ohio State: Bob Knight attended Ohio State University and played college basketball for the Ohio State Buckeyes. He was a part of the team during the late 1950s and early 1960s.

National Championship: One of the highlights of Knight's college playing career was his involvement in the Ohio State team that won the NCAA national championship in 1960. The Buckeyes, led by head coach Fred Taylor, defeated California in the championship game.

Position: Knight primarily played the role of a reserve player and was known for his defensive skills and basketball IQ. While he didn't have a prominent scoring role, his contributions on the court were valued by his team.

All-Academic Honors: In addition to his basketball skills, Knight was an excellent student. He was named an Academic All-American during his college years, reflecting his commitment to both academics and athletics.

Teammates: Knight played alongside fellow Ohio State basketball greats such as Jerry Lucas and John Havlicek, who went on to have successful careers in the NBA.

Bob Knight's college playing career at Ohio State was marked by his role as a defensive specialist and his contributions to a championship-winning team. While he is more widely recognized for his coaching career, his time as a college player laid the foundation for his deep understanding of the game of basketball and his eventual success as a coach.

2:2 CHILDHOOD

Bob Knight's childhood was marked by his upbringing in Massillon, Ohio, and his early experiences that contributed to his passion for basketball. Here are some insights into his childhood:

Humble Beginnings: Bob Knight was raised in a working-class family. His father, Clevenger Knight, worked as a welder, and his mother, Hazel Knight, was a homemaker. They instilled in him the values of hard work and discipline from an early age.

Love for Basketball: Knight's love for basketball began in his childhood. He was introduced to the sport at a young age and quickly developed a passion for it. This passion would become a driving force in his life.

Orrville High School: Knight attended Orrville High School in Orrville, Ohio. It was during his high school years that he started to make a name for himself as a talented basketball player.

Academic Excellence: Alongside his athletic pursuits, Knight excelled academically. He was a dedicated student and, upon graduation, was named valedictorian of his class in 1958.

Early Influence: During his childhood and formative years, Knight was influenced by coaches, teachers, and mentors who played a significant role in shaping his approach to the game and instilling values of hard work, discipline, and attention to detail.

These early experiences in Massillon, Ohio, set the stage for Bob Knight's future success in basketball, both as a player and, more notably, as a coach. His childhood taught him the importance of hard work, a commitment to excellence, and the value of education, all of which became integral to his life and career in basketball.

2:3 COLLEGE BASKETBALL CAREER

Bob Knight's college basketball career at Ohio State University was an integral part of his journey in the sport. Here are some key details about his time playing for the Ohio State Buckeyes:

Enrollment at Ohio State: Bob Knight attended Ohio State University and played for the Ohio State Buckeyes during the late 1950s and early 1960s.

Position and Playing Style: Knight was a reserve player during his college career. He was known for his defensive skills, basketball IQ, and court awareness. While he wasn't a high-scoring player, his contributions on the defensive end and his understanding of the game were highly valued.

1960 NCAA Championship: One of the most significant achievements of Bob Knight's college playing career was winning the NCAA national championship in 1960. The Ohio State Buckeyes, coached by Fred Taylor, secured the national title by defeating California in the championship game.

Teammates: Knight played alongside talented teammates, including Jerry Lucas and John Havlicek, who would go on to have successful careers in the NBA. The combination of Knight's defensive skills and the offensive prowess of his teammates contributed to the success of the Buckeyes.

Academic Excellence: In addition to his basketball pursuits, Bob Knight maintained a strong focus on academics. He was named an Academic All-American during his college years, highlighting his dedication to both sports and education.

Bob Knight's college playing career at Ohio State University laid the foundation for his deep understanding of the game of basketball and contributed to his future success as a coach. Winning the NCAA championship was a significant achievement, and his ability to balance athletics and academics reflected his commitment to excellence on and off the court.

CHAPTER 3, COACHING CAREER BEGIN

Bob Knight's coaching career is one of the most iconic and polarizing in the history of college basketball. Here's an overview of his coaching career, highlighting some of the key points and milestones:

Early Coaching Experience: Bob Knight's coaching career began during his service in the United States Army. He served as an assistant coach for the Army Black Knights' basketball team. This marked the start of his coaching journey.

**Indiana University (1971-2000): Knight's most prominent coaching tenure was at Indiana University, where he served as the head coach from 1971 to 2000. During this time, he achieved remarkable success, winning three NCAA national championships (in 1976, 1981, and 1987). The Hoosiers also claimed numerous Big Ten conference titles under his leadership.

Coaching Philosophy: Knight was known for his disciplined and structured coaching style. He emphasized strong defense, teamwork, and attention to fundamentals. His "motion offense" and "motion defense" became hallmarks of his coaching philosophy.

Controversies: Knight's coaching career was marred by various controversies, including his confrontational and, at times, aggressive behavior. His actions led to several disciplinary incidents, fines, and suspensions. Ultimately, in 2000, he was dismissed from his position at Indiana University due to a widely publicized altercation with a student.

Texas Tech University (2001-2008): Following his departure from Indiana, Bob Knight continued his coaching career at Texas Tech University. He coached the Texas Tech Red Raiders from 2001 to 2008. While at Texas Tech, Knight achieved notable successes and further solidified his status as a coaching legend.

Retirement: Bob Knight retired from coaching in February 2008. His career as a coach spanned several decades and left an indelible mark on college basketball.

Broadcasting Career: After retiring from coaching, Knight transitioned into broadcasting and provided commentary on college basketball. His insights and perspectives on the game continued to be of interest to basketball fans.

Bob Knight's coaching career is remembered for his incredible success on the court, his influence on coaching philosophy, and his complex personality. While celebrated for his achievements, he also faced criticism and controversy due to his confrontational coaching style. His impact on the sport of college basketball and the players he coached remains significant and enduring.

3:1 EARLY COACHING EXPERIENCE

Bob Knight's early coaching experience began during his service in the United States Army, which served as a stepping stone for his future career in coaching. Here are the key details of his early coaching experiences:

Assistant Coach at Army: While serving in the Army, Bob Knight was assigned to the United States Military Academy at West Point, where he took on the role of an assistant coach for the Army Black Knights' basketball team.

Mentorship and Learning: Knight worked under the head coach, Tates Locke, and gained valuable coaching experience during his time at West Point. He absorbed coaching strategies, leadership skills, and basketball knowledge that would later become instrumental in his coaching career.

Introduction to Discipline: It was during this early coaching experience that Knight further developed his coaching philosophy, emphasizing discipline, attention to fundamentals, and a strong work ethic. These principles would become the cornerstones of his coaching style.

Transition to High School Coaching: After his service in the Army, Bob Knight began his high school coaching career. He served as the head basketball coach at Cuyahoga Falls High School in Ohio. This experience allowed him to continue honing his coaching skills and working with young players.

Bob Knight's early coaching experiences, both as an assistant coach at West Point and later as a high school head coach, laid the foundation for his successful coaching career in college basketball. The principles of discipline and strong fundamentals that he adopted during this period would become defining features of his coaching philosophy as he went on to coach at the collegiate level.

3:2 ARRIVAL AS UNITED STATE ARMY HEAD COACH

Bob Knight's arrival at the United States Military Academy at West Point as the head coach of the Army Black Knights' basketball team marked a significant milestone in his coaching career. Here's an overview of his transition to this role:

Assistant Coach at Army: As mentioned earlier, Bob Knight started his coaching career as an assistant coach for the Army Black Knights' basketball team while he was serving in the United States Army. He gained valuable coaching experience and knowledge during this time.

Promotion to Head Coach: In 1965, Knight was promoted to the position of head coach of the Army basketball team, a role he would hold for five seasons. This promotion provided him with the opportunity to lead a collegiate basketball program.

Coaching Style and Discipline: Knight brought his strong coaching philosophy centered on discipline, hard work, and attention to fundamentals to the Army team. These principles were integral to his coaching style and contributed to the success he would achieve in his future coaching career.

Developing Players: Knight's coaching at Army helped him develop and mentor young players. He focused on improving their skills, both on and off the court, which became a hallmark of his coaching career.

Transition to Indiana University: Knight's success at Army caught the attention of Indiana University, and in 1971, he made a significant move in his coaching career by becoming the head coach of the Indiana Hoosiers. This marked the beginning of a highly successful and, at times, controversial coaching journey at the collegiate level.

Bob Knight's time as the head coach at Army was a crucial phase in his development as a basketball coach. His coaching principles and the discipline he instilled in his players laid the groundwork for his future coaching success, both at Indiana University and later at Texas Tech University.

CHAPTER 4, INDIANA HOOSIERS ERA

Bob Knight's era as the head coach of the Indiana Hoosiers is one of the most celebrated and storied periods in the history of college basketball. Here's an overview of his time at Indiana University:

1. Hiring at Indiana University: Bob Knight was hired as the head coach of the Indiana Hoosiers in 1971, succeeding Lou Watson. This marked the beginning of a remarkable coaching journey at one of college basketball's most prestigious programs.

2. Immediate Success: Knight's tenure at Indiana University got off to a fast start. In just his third season, he led the Hoosiers to the 1976 NCAA national championship, a significant achievement in his coaching career.

3. Championships and Successes: Under Knight's leadership, the Indiana Hoosiers won a total of three NCAA national championships during his tenure, with

additional titles in 1981 and 1987. The team also secured numerous Big Ten conference titles.

4. **Coaching Philosophy:** Knight was known for his disciplined coaching style. He emphasized strong defense, teamwork, and attention to fundamentals. His "motion offense" and "motion defense" became synonymous with Indiana basketball and were central to his coaching philosophy.

5. **Notable Players:** Knight coached and developed numerous standout players during his time at Indiana, including stars like Isiah Thomas, Kent Benson, and Steve Alford. These players went on to have successful careers in the NBA.

6. Conflicts and Discipline: Despite the on-court success, Knight's tenure was marked by controversies and disciplinary incidents. His confrontational coaching style and behavior led to several controversies, suspensions, and fines.

7. **Departure from Indiana:** In September 2000, after a highly publicized incident involving a confrontation with

a student, Bob Knight was dismissed from his position as the head coach of the Indiana Hoosiers. His departure marked the end of an era in Indiana basketball.

Bob Knight's time at Indiana University left an indelible mark on the world of college basketball. He was a coaching legend known for his achievements, his unique coaching style, and his complex personality. His success and controversies during his Indiana Hoosiers era continue to be a subject of fascination and debate in the basketball community.

4:1 CHAMPIONSHIP

Bob Knight, the legendary basketball coach, achieved remarkable success during his coaching career, particularly in terms of winning NCAA national championships. Here are the NCAA national championships won by Bob Knight as a head coach:

1. 1976 NCAA National Championship: In just his fifth season as the head coach of the Indiana Hoosiers, Bob Knight led the team to an NCAA national championship in 1976. The Hoosiers had a remarkable season and secured the title by defeating the University of Michigan in the championship game.

2. 1981 NCAA National Championship: Five years after his first championship, Knight guided the Indiana Hoosiers to another NCAA national championship in 1981. The team's memorable run included defeating the University of North Carolina in the championship game.

3. 1987 NCAA National Championship: Bob Knight's third and final NCAA national championship as a head coach came in 1987. The Indiana Hoosiers, led by outstanding players like Steve Alford, clinched the championship by defeating Syracuse University in the title game.

These three NCAA national championships stand as significant highlights of Bob Knight's coaching career and have solidified his legacy as one of the most successful and influential college basketball coaches in history. His coaching philosophy, disciplined style, and ability to lead his teams to championship victories remain part of his enduring legacy in the sport.

4:2 SUCCESSES

Bob Knight, throughout his coaching career, achieved a wide range of successes and milestones. Here are some of the notable successes and accomplishments associated with Bob Knight:

1. **NCAA National Championships:** Knight won three NCAA national championships as a head coach. These championships came in 1976, 1981, and 1987, while he was leading the Indiana Hoosiers.

2. **Conference Titles:** Knight's teams claimed numerous Big Ten conference titles during his coaching career. Winning the conference championship was a consistent achievement throughout his time at Indiana.

3. Development of Players: Knight was renowned for developing his players' skills and helping them reach their full potential. Many of his former players, such as Isiah Thomas, Kent Benson, and Steve Alford, had successful careers in the NBA.

4. Disciplined Coaching Style: Knight's disciplined coaching style, emphasizing strong defense and teamwork, influenced the basketball world. His "motion offense" and "motion defense" strategies became widely recognized and adopted by coaches at all levels.

5. **Mentorship:** Knight served as a mentor to many coaches who later had successful careers, including Mike Krzyzewski (Coach K) and Pat Riley.

6. Broadcasting Career: After retiring from coaching, Bob Knight transitioned into broadcasting and provided insightful commentary on college basketball. His contributions to the broadcasting world added value to the coverage of the sport.

7. Academic All-Americans: Knight's emphasis on academics led to several of his players being named

Academic All-Americans, demonstrating his commitment to both education and athletics.

8. Influence on Coaching Philosophy: His impact on coaching philosophy, leadership, and management has been studied and adapted in various fields beyond basketball.

It's important to note that while Bob Knight achieved remarkable success in his coaching career, it was also marked by controversies and disciplinary incidents. His legacy is multifaceted, with both accolades and criticisms, making him a polarizing figure in the world of sports.

4:3 CONTROVERSIES

Bob Knight's coaching career was marked by several controversies and disciplinary incidents. Here are some of the notable controversies and incidents associated with Bob Knight:

1. Confrontational Coaching Style: Bob Knight was known for his fiery and confrontational coaching style. He often engaged in heated exchanges with referees, players, and even fans. These confrontations sometimes led to ejections and fines.

2. Chair-throwing incident: One of the most infamous incidents involving Bob Knight occurred in 1985, when he threw a chair onto the court during a game. This act of anger resulted in a one-game suspension.

3. Player Altercations: Knight had a reputation for being tough on his players. There were reports of physical altercations between Knight and his players, which raised concerns about his coaching methods.

4. **Verbal Outbursts:** Knight's verbal outbursts and profanity-laden tirades, often directed at players and officials, were widely publicized and criticized. These incidents strained his relationships with many individuals in the basketball world.

5. Dismissal from Indiana University: In 2000, Bob Knight was dismissed from his position as the head

coach of the Indiana Hoosiers. His dismissal was a result of a highly publicized confrontation with a student, which violated the university's "zero-tolerance" policy for his behavior.

6. **Controversial Comments:** Knight was also known for making controversial and insensitive remarks in interviews and public appearances. His comments sometimes drew criticism and backlash.

7. Interaction with Media: Knight had a contentious relationship with the media. He was known for being uncooperative and often hostile in his interactions with reporters and journalists.

These controversies and disciplinary incidents, along with his confrontational coaching style, contributed to the polarizing nature of Bob Knight's career. While he achieved significant success as a coach, these incidents continue to be part of his legacy and are often discussed in assessments of his impact on the basketball world.

4:4 DISCIPLINARY ACTIONS

Bob Knight's coaching career was marked by a number of disciplinary actions and consequences for his behavior. Here are some of the notable disciplinary actions and sanctions that he faced during his coaching career:

1. Chair-Throwing Incident (1985): In 1985, during a game, Bob Knight famously threw a chair onto the court in a display of frustration. This act led to a one-game suspension and a fine for his behavior.

2. Verbal Abuse and Ejections: Knight was often ejected from games for engaging in heated arguments and confrontations with referees. These incidents resulted in suspensions and fines.

3. Physical Altercations with Players: There were reports of physical altercations between Knight and some of his players, including instances where he grabbed or

pushed them. These incidents raised concerns about his coaching methods.

4. Dismissal from Indiana University (2000): In 2000, Bob Knight was dismissed from his position as the head coach of the Indiana Hoosiers by the university's administration. His dismissal was a result of a confrontation with a student that violated the university's "zero-tolerance" policy for his behavior. This marked the end of his tenure at Indiana.

5. Suspensions and Fines: Throughout his coaching career, Knight faced suspensions and fines imposed by the NCAA, the Big Ten Conference, and the institutions he coached. These penalties were a consequence of his behavior and actions on and off the court.

6. **Controversial Comments:** Knight made controversial and insensitive comments in interviews and public appearances. While these comments didn't always result in disciplinary actions, they often drew criticism and backlash from the public and media.

These disciplinary actions and sanctions, in addition to his confrontational coaching style, contributed to the polarizing nature of Bob Knight's career. While he achieved significant success as a coach, his behavior and disciplinary incidents continue to be part of his legacy and are subjects of ongoing discussion and debate.

CHAPTER 5, TRANSITION TO TEXAS TECH

Bob Knight's transition to Texas Tech University marked a significant chapter in his coaching career. Here's an overview of his move to Texas Tech:

Indian University Departure: Bob Knight's tenure at Indiana University came to an end in September 2000 when he was dismissed from his position as head coach due to a high-profile altercation with a student. His departure from Indiana marked the end of an era in college basketball.

Texas Tech Appointment: In March 2001, just a few months after leaving Indiana, Bob Knight was appointed as the head coach of the Texas Tech Red Raiders His arrival at Texas Tech generated considerable attention and excitement in the college basketball world.

Coaching at Texas Tech: Bob Knight took over the Texas Tech basketball program with the aim of revitalizing the team's competitiveness. During his time at Texas Tech, he made significant contributions to the program, helping the Red Raiders achieve success and respectability in the Big 12 Conference.

Success at Texas Tech: Knight's tenure at Texas Tech was marked by notable achievements, including leading the Red Raiders to several NCAA tournament appearances. His coaching acumen and disciplined style had a positive impact on the program.

Retirement from Coaching: In February 2008, Bob Knight announced his retirement from coaching during the middle of the 2007–2008 season. His retirement marked the end of his active coaching career.

Continued Involvement in Basketball: After retiring from coaching, Bob Knight remained involved in the world of basketball through broadcasting, providing commentary and insights on the sport.

Bob Knight's transition to Texas Tech allowed him to continue his coaching career and leave his mark on another college basketball program. His time at Texas Tech added to his coaching legacy and solidified his status as one of the most iconic figures in the history of the sport.

5:1 COACHING TEXAS TECH RED RAIDERS

Bob Knight's coaching tenure with the Texas Tech Red Raiders was a significant period in his career and left a lasting impact on the program. Here's an overview of his coaching stint with the Texas Tech Red Raiders:

Appointment as Head Coach: Bob Knight was appointed as the head coach of the Texas Tech Red Raiders in March 2001, shortly after leaving Indiana University. His hiring generated a lot of excitement and attention, as he brought a wealth of coaching experience and a strong reputation to Texas Tech.

Resurgence of the Program: When Knight arrived at Texas Tech, the basketball program was in need of revitalization. He quickly implemented his disciplined coaching style and emphasis on fundamentals, which had been hallmarks of his coaching philosophy throughout his career.

Success and NCAA Tournament Appearances: Under Knight's leadership, the Red Raiders experienced a resurgence. They made multiple appearances in the NCAA tournament, a significant accomplishment for the program. His coaching acumen and ability to develop players contributed to the team's success.

Student-Athlete Development: Bob Knight's focus on player development and the emphasis on academics were evident at Texas Tech. He continued to mentor and develop young athletes, both on and off the court.

Legacy and Impact: Knight's time at Texas Tech further solidified his status as a coaching legend. His contributions to the program and the broader basketball community were widely recognized. He had a positive influence on his players and left a lasting legacy at the university.

Retirement from Coaching: In February 2008, Bob Knight announced his retirement from coaching during the middle of the 2007–2008 season. His retirement marked the end of his active coaching career, but he remained connected to the sport through broadcasting and commentary work.

Bob Knight's coaching tenure with the Texas Tech Red Raiders showcased his ability to make a meaningful impact on a program in need of transformation. His disciplined coaching style, focus on fundamentals, and commitment to player development were evident throughout his time at Texas Tech, and he played a vital role in the program's success and growth.

5:2 ACHIEVEMENTS

Bob Knight's coaching tenure with the Texas Tech Red Raiders was marked by several significant achievements and contributions to the program. Here are some of his notable accomplishments during his time at Texas Tech:

Resurgence of the Program: When Bob Knight arrived at Texas Tech, the basketball program was in need of revitalization. Under his leadership, the Red Raiders experienced a resurgence in competitiveness and performance.

NCAA Tournament Appearances: Knight's coaching acumen helped Texas Tech make multiple appearances in the NCAA tournament during his tenure. These tournament appearances were a testament to the team's improved performance.

Winning Seasons: The Red Raiders had winning seasons under Knight's guidance, consistently achieving a positive win-loss record.

Player Development: Knight continued his emphasis on player development at Texas Tech, helping athletes improve their skills and prepare for the next level of basketball.

Improved Defense: Bob Knight's commitment to strong defensive play was evident in the team's improved defensive performance during his time at Texas Tech.

Positive Influence on Players: Knight's disciplined coaching style had a positive impact on the players he coached, helping them develop both as athletes and as individuals.

Respectability in the Big 12 Conference: Texas Tech gained respectability in the highly competitive Big 12 Conference during Knight's tenure. The team was seen as a more competitive and formidable opponent.

Bob Knight's achievements at Texas Tech were characterized by a renewed sense of competitiveness and a commitment to fundamentals and defense. His influence extended beyond the basketball court, and his contributions to the program helped lay the foundation for future success.

CHAPTER 6, LEGACY OF COACHING STYLE

Bob Knight's coaching style and legacy in this regard have had a lasting impact on the world of basketball. Here are some key elements of his coaching style and his legacy:

Discipline and Accountability: Knight was known for instilling discipline in his players and holding them accountable for their actions on and off the court. He demanded a high level of commitment and work ethic from his athletes.

Attention to Fundamentals: Knight's coaching philosophy placed a strong emphasis on the fundamentals of basketball. He believed that mastering the basics, such as passing, shooting, and defensive positioning, was crucial to success.

Motion Offense and Defense: He popularized the "motion offense" and "motion defense" strategies, which emphasized fluid movement, spacing, and teamwork on the court. These systems are still studied and used in basketball coaching.

Defensive Focus: Knight's teams were known for their strong defensive play. He emphasized the importance of defense and taught his players how to effectively guard their opponents.

Player Development: Knight had a reputation for developing his players' skills and basketball IQ. Many of his former players went on to have successful careers in the NBA, which reflected his influence as a mentor and teacher.

Demanding Work Ethic: Knight's coaching style was characterized by a demanding work ethic. He expected his players to give their best effort in practice and games and pushed them to reach their full potential.

Legacy in Coaching Philosophy: Bob Knight's coaching style and principles continue to be studied and emulated by basketball coaches at various levels. His influence can be seen in the coaching philosophies of many successful coaches who have adopted elements of his approach.

Controversy and Polarizing Nature: It's important to note that while Knight's coaching style left a significant legacy, it was also marked by controversies, confrontational behavior, and disciplinary incidents. This polarizing aspect of his coaching career is an integral part of his legacy.

Bob Knight's coaching style, with its focus on discipline, fundamentals, and defense, has had a lasting impact on the game of basketball. His legacy is seen in the many players and coaches who have been influenced by his teachings and in the enduring principles of his coaching philosophy.

6:1 COACHING PHILOSOPHY

Bob Knight's coaching philosophy was built on several key principles and philosophies that guided his approach to coaching. Here are the fundamental elements of Bob Knight's coaching philosophy:

Discipline: Discipline was at the core of Knight's coaching philosophy. He believed in instilling discipline in his players, emphasizing punctuality, hard work, and adherence to team rules. He demanded a high level of commitment and accountability from his athletes.

Fundamentals: Knight placed a strong emphasis on the fundamentals of basketball. He believed that mastering the basics, such as passing, shooting, dribbling, and defensive positioning, was crucial to success. He advocated for consistent and precise execution of these fundamental skills.

Motion Offense: Knight is renowned for popularizing the "motion offense." This system emphasized constant player movement, good spacing, and teamwork on the court. Players were encouraged to read and react to the defense, leading to a fluid and flexible offensive strategy.

Motion Defense: Similarly, Knight's "motion defense" focused on active, man-to-man defensive play. It required players to work together to deny their opponents opportunities and make smart decisions on the court.

Strong Work Ethics: Knight expected his players to have a strong work ethic. He believed that hard work and dedication were essential for success in both practice and games.

Attention to Detail: Knight was known for his meticulous attention to detail. He believed that success in basketball, as in life, often came down to the little things. He coached his players to be precise in their execution.

Player Development: Knight was dedicated to developing his players' skills and basketball IQ. He took on the role of mentor and teacher, helping his athletes reach their full potential.

Demand for Excellence: Knight had a reputation for demanding excellence from his players. He pushed them to give their best effort, both individually and as a team.

Strong Defense: Knight's teams were often characterized by their strong defensive play. He taught his players the importance of defense and how to effectively guard their opponents.

Education and Academics: Knight placed value on education and academics. He encouraged his players to excel in the classroom as well as on the court and emphasized the importance of being well-rounded individuals.

Conflict and Accountability: While his coaching philosophy emphasized discipline and accountability,

Knight's confrontational coaching style and controversial behavior were also part of his legacy.

Bob Knight's coaching philosophy left a significant mark on the world of basketball. His emphasis on discipline, fundamentals, and attention to detail, along with his commitment to player development, influenced generations of coaches and players: His legacy, while multifaceted, continues to be a subject of study and discussion in the basketball community.

6:2 INFLUENCE ON BASKETBALL

Bob Knight's influence on the world of basketball is significant and far-reaching. His coaching career, coaching philosophy, and approach to the game have left a lasting impact on various aspects of basketball. Here are some of the ways in which Bob Knight influenced the sport:

Coaching Philosophy: Knight's disciplined coaching style, emphasis on fundamentals, and meticulous attention to detail have had a profound influence on coaching at all levels of basketball. Coaches have adopted elements of his philosophy to develop their own coaching styles.

Motion Offense and Defense: Knight's "motion offense" and "motion defense" strategies have become integral components of many basketball programs. These systems, which prioritize player movement, spacing, and teamwork, continue to be used and studied in coaching circles.

Player Development: Knight's commitment to player development and mentorship has left a lasting impact. His focus on improving players' skills and basketball IQ has been adopted by coaches who aim to help athletes reach their full potential.

Strong Defense: Knight's emphasis on strong defense and man-to-man play has influenced defensive strategies in basketball. Coaches continue to teach and prioritize sound defensive principles inspired by his approach.

Commitment to Discipline and Work Ethics: Knight's legacy of discipline and a strong work ethic continues to be an important part of basketball coaching. These values are often instilled in players as they develop their skills and character.

Academics and Student-Athlete Success: Knight's emphasis on education and academics has contributed to the development of well-rounded student-athletes. Coaches recognize the importance of academic success alongside athletic achievement.

Mentorship: Many of Knight's former players and assistant coaches have gone on to have successful coaching careers, passing on the knowledge and principles they gained from him.

Broadcasting and Analysis: After retiring from coaching, Knight transitioned into broadcasting and provided commentary on college basketball. His insights and perspectives continued to contribute to our understanding of the game.

Complex Legacy: Knight's controversial and polarizing coaching style has also had an influence, sparking discussions and debates about the role of intensity and behavior in sports.

Iconic Figure: Knight remains an iconic and recognizable figure in the sport of basketball, and his name is often associated with the history of the game.

Bob Knight's impact on basketball extends beyond the Xs and Os of the game. His principles and legacy continue to shape coaching, player development, and the broader basketball community, making him a highly influential figure in the sport's history.

CHAPTER 7, PERSONAL LIFE

Bob Knight is widely recognized for his coaching career and his impact on the world of basketball. He also had a personal life that included various aspects:

Family: Bob Knight was married to his wife, Karen Vieth Edgar, and they had two sons, Tim and Pat Knight.

Hobbies and Interests: Outside of basketball, Knight had diverse interests. He was an avid fly fisherman and enjoyed spending time outdoors. He also had a passion for history and military strategy.

Academic Pursuits: Knight had a strong commitment to education and was known for his interest in history and military history. He was a voracious reader and often recommended books to his players.

Controversies: Knight's personal life was at times overshadowed by controversies, particularly related to his confrontational coaching style and disciplinary incidents. These controversies often made headlines and were a part of his personal and public life.

Retirement: After retiring from coaching, Knight continued to stay involved in basketball through broadcasting. He provided commentary and analysis on college basketball, which allowed him to remain connected to the sport.

Health: In his later years, Knight faced health challenges, including issues related to his heart. His health became a subject of concern among his supporters and the basketball community.

Bob Knight's personal life, like his coaching career, was marked by both accomplishments and controversies. While he was celebrated for his success on the basketball court, his personality and behavior were a subject of fascination and debate, making him a complex and polarizing figure in both his personal and public life.

7:1 OFF-COURT INCIDENT

Bob Knight was involved in various off-court incidents and controversies throughout his career. Some of these incidents received significant media attention and were widely discussed. Here are a few notable off-court incidents involving Bob Knight:

**Dismissal from Indiana University (2000): One of the most significant off-court incidents in Knight's career was his dismissal from Indiana University in 2000. He was let go as the head coach of the Indiana Hoosiers following a highly publicized altercation with a student. This altercation violated the university's "zero-tolerance" policy for his behavior.

Chair-Throwing Incident (1985): During a game in 1985, Bob Knight famously threw a chair onto the court in a display of frustration. This act led to a one-game suspension and a fine for his behavior.

Confrontations and Altercations: Knight had numerous confrontations and altercations with referees, players, and fans over the years. These incidents often resulted in ejections and disciplinary actions.

Controversial Comments: Knight was known for making controversial and insensitive comments in interviews and public appearances. These comments sometimes drew criticism and backlash from the public and media.

Media and Journalist Relations: Knight had a contentious relationship with the media. He was known for being uncooperative and often hostile in his interactions with reporters and journalists.

These off-court incidents and controversies, combined with his confrontational coaching style, contributed to the polarizing nature of Bob Knight's career. While he was celebrated for his coaching achievements, his behavior off the court was a subject of discussion and debate throughout his career.

CHAPTER 8, POST COACHING CAREER

After retiring from coaching, Bob Knight transitioned into a different phase of his life and remained active in various pursuits. Here are some of the key activities and aspects of Bob Knight's post-coaching career:

1. **Broadcasting:** Bob Knight became a basketball commentator and analyst, offering insights and commentary on college basketball. He provided his expertise and perspectives on the game through various media outlets, contributing to the coverage and analysis of college basketball.

2. **Public Speaking:** Knight engaged in public speaking and made appearances at events where he shared his experiences and knowledge in the world of basketball. He often spoke about leadership, teamwork, and his coaching philosophy.

3. **Authorship:** Knight wrote several books related to basketball and coaching. His books included "Knight: My Story" and "The Power of Negative Thinking: An

Unconventional Approach to Achieving Positive Results."

4. Community Involvement: He remained active in his local community and continued to participate in charitable and community-oriented activities.

5. Personal Interests: Knight pursued his personal interests, including fishing and reading. He was known for being an avid fly fisherman and had a passion for history and military strategy.

6. Health Challenges: In his later years, Bob Knight faced health challenges, including heart-related issues. His health became a subject of concern among his supporters and the basketball community.

7. **Family:** Knight spent time with his family and enjoyed personal moments with his wife, children, and grandchildren.

Bob Knight's post-coaching career allowed him to remain connected to the world of basketball through broadcasting and other basketball-related activities.

While he transitioned into a different role, his contributions to the sport continued, and he remained a prominent figure in the basketball community.

8:1 RETIREMENT

Bob Knight officially announced his retirement from coaching during the middle of the 2007–2008 college basketball season. His retirement marked the end of a long and storied coaching career. Here are the key details surrounding Bob Knight's retirement:

1. **Retirement Announcement:** In February 2008, Bob Knight made the decision to retire from coaching. The announcement came during his tenure as head coach of the Texas Tech Red Raiders.

2. Mid-Season Retirement: Knight's retirement announcement was somewhat unusual in that it occurred in the middle of the basketball season. He chose to step down from his coaching position before the season had concluded.

3. End of Active Coaching Career: Bob Knight's retirement signified the conclusion of his active coaching career, which had spanned several decades and included successful tenures at Indiana University and Texas Tech University.

4. **Legacy:** His retirement marked the end of an era in college basketball, as Knight was widely regarded as one of the sport's most iconic and influential coaches. His legacy, coaching philosophy, and contributions to the game continued to be celebrated and analyzed by the basketball community.

5. Transition to Broadcasting: After retiring from coaching, Knight transitioned to a broadcasting career, where he provided commentary and analysis on college basketball. His insights and perspectives added value to the coverage of the sport.

Bob Knight's retirement from coaching was a significant moment in the world of college basketball. While it marked the end of his active coaching career, his impact on the sport and his presence in the basketball community remained strong through his work in broadcasting and his enduring legacy as a coaching legend.

8:2 LIFE AFTER COACHING

After retiring from coaching, Bob Knight transitioned to a different phase of his life, which included various activities and interests. Here's an overview of Bob Knight's life after coaching:

1. **Broadcasting:** Following his coaching career, Knight became a basketball commentator and analyst. He provided insights and commentary on college basketball through various media outlets. His extensive knowledge and unique perspective made him a valuable addition to the broadcasting world.

2. **Public Speaking:** Bob Knight engaged in public speaking engagements. He made appearances at events where he shared his experiences and wisdom in

the world of basketball. His speeches often touched on leadership, teamwork, and his coaching philosophy.

3. **Authorship:** Knight authored several books related to basketball, leadership, and coaching. His books included titles like "Knight: My Story" and "The Power of Negative Thinking: An Unconventional Approach to Achieving Positive Results."

4. Community Involvement: He remained involved in his local community and participated in charitable and community-oriented activities. His contributions extended beyond the basketball court.

5. Personal Interests: Knight pursued his personal interests and hobbies, including fishing and reading. He was known for his passion for fly fishing and his interest in history and military strategy.

6. **Health:** In his later years, Knight faced health challenges, including heart-related issues. His health became a matter of concern among his supporters and the basketball community.

7. Family: Knight spent time with his family, including his wife, children, and grandchildren, enjoying personal moments and family gatherings.

Bob Knight's life after coaching allowed him to remain connected to the world of basketball through broadcasting and other basketball-related activities. He continued to share his knowledge and experiences with a broader audience and left a lasting mark on the sport even after retiring from coaching.

8:3 BROADCAST WORK

After retiring from coaching, Bob Knight transitioned into a broadcasting career, where he provided commentary and analysis on college basketball. His insights and perspectives as a seasoned coach added depth to the coverage of the sport. Here are some details about Bob Knight's broadcasting career:

1. Basketball Commentator: Knight served as a basketball commentator and analyst for various media

outlets, including television networks that covered college basketball games. He offered his expertise, insights, and opinions on the teams, players, and strategies involved in the sport.

2. Analysis and Insights: Knight's role as a commentator allowed him to provide in-depth analysis of the games, players' performances, coaching strategies, and the overall dynamics of college basketball. His unique perspective as a legendary coach was highly valued by basketball enthusiasts.

3. Television Appearances: He made regular appearances on college basketball broadcasts, including games, pre-game and post-game shows, and halftime analysis segments. His contributions enhanced the viewing experience for fans.

4. Contributions to Broadcasting: Knight's presence in broadcasting extended his influence in the world of basketball. His extensive knowledge of the sport and his reputation as a coaching icon made him a respected figure in the field of sports broadcasting.

5. Retirement from Broadcasting: Over time, Bob Knight reduced his broadcasting commitments, eventually retiring from his role as a basketball commentator. His contributions to broadcasting left a lasting legacy and enriched the coverage of college basketball.

Bob Knight's transition to broadcasting allowed him to continue his involvement in the sport he loved while offering fans and viewers valuable insights and analysis from a coach's perspective. His broadcasting career was an extension of his lifelong connection to basketball.

8:4 COMMENTARY WORK

Bob Knight's commentary work in the world of basketball involved providing analysis, insights, and opinions on college basketball games and related events. His extensive coaching experience and knowledge of the sport made him a valuable commentator and analyst. Here are some key aspects of Bob Knight's commentary work:

1. Game Analysis: Knight offered an in-depth analysis of college basketball games. He commented on the strategies employed by teams, the execution of plays, and the performance of individual players.

2. Coaching Insights: His commentary often included insights into coaching strategies, emphasizing the importance of fundamentals, defensive play, and teamwork. He shared his coaching philosophy with viewers.

3. Player Evaluation: Knight provided assessments of players' skills, strengths, and weaknesses. His analysis drew on his ability to identify key aspects of a player's performance.

4. Historical Perspective: Given his passion for history and military strategy, Knight occasionally incorporated historical analogies and references to illustrate his points and make the game more relatable.

5. **Candid Commentary:** Knight was known for his straightforward and candid commentary. He expressed

his opinions openly and did not shy away from providing critical feedback when necessary.

6. Pre-game and Halftime Shows: In addition to game analysis, Knight often appeared on pre-game and halftime shows, offering previews and recaps of games and providing additional context to enhance viewers' understanding of the matchups.

7. Broadcasting Outlets: Knight worked for various television networks and broadcasting outlets that covered college basketball, including ESPN and other sports networks.

8. **Retirement from Commentary:** Over time, Bob Knight reduced his commitments to broadcasting, ultimately retiring from his role as a basketball commentator. His contributions to commentary and analysis enriched the college basketball viewing experience for fans.

Bob Knight's commentary work was an extension of his lifelong passion for basketball and his desire to share his knowledge with a broader audience. His insights and perspectives as a legendary coach added value to the coverage of college basketball games and events.

CHAPTER 9, IMPACT ON PLAYERS

Bob Knight had a significant impact on the players he coached throughout his storied career. His influence went beyond the basketball court, shaping the lives of many athletes both as players and as individuals. Here are some key ways in which Bob Knight impacted his players:

Player Development: Knight was known for his ability to develop players' basketball skills. Many of his former players went on to have successful careers in the NBA and other professional leagues. His coaching helped them reach their full potential.

Emphasis on Fundamentals: Knight's coaching philosophy stressed the importance of mastering the fundamentals of the game. He instilled a strong foundation of basketball skills in his players, which served them well throughout their careers.

Work Ethic and Discipline: He demanded a strong work ethic and discipline from his players. Knight's coaching style taught players the value of hard work, commitment, and dedication to their craft.

Teamwork: Knight emphasized the importance of teamwork and unselfish play. His players learned how to work together, both on and off the court, to achieve their goals.

Life Skills: Knight's mentorship extended beyond basketball. He often provided life lessons and guidance to his players, helping them become well-rounded individuals and better citizens.

Academic Success: He emphasized the importance of academics and encouraged his players to excel in the classroom as well as on the court. Many of his players achieved academic success and became Academic All-Americans.

Leadership Skills: Knight's coaching helped players develop leadership skills, as they often had to take on leadership roles within the team. Many of his former players went on to become leaders in their respective careers.

Mentorship: Knight served as a mentor to many of his players, offering guidance and support throughout their lives. His impact on their personal and professional development extended long after their playing days were over.

Respect for the Game: Knight instilled a deep respect for the game of basketball in his players. His coaching and philosophy emphasized the traditions and integrity of the sport.

Lasting Relationships: Many of Knight's former players maintained close and enduring relationships with their coach. They often spoke fondly of the impact he had on their lives.

While Bob Knight's coaching style was often intense and demanding, his players recognized the lasting positive effects of his mentorship and coaching. His impact on their lives extended far beyond the basketball court, shaping them into successful athletes and individuals.

9:1 STORIES AND TESTIMONIALS FROM FORMER PLAYERS

Former players of Bob Knight, both from Indiana University and Texas Tech University, have shared stories and testimonials that provide insights into their experiences with the legendary coach. Here are a few examples:

Isaac Thomas (Indiana University): Isiah Thomas, who played for Knight at Indiana University, has spoken about the valuable life lessons he learned from Knight. He has praised Knight's coaching as instrumental in his development, not only as a player but as a person.

Steve Alford (Indiana University): Steve Alford, who played for Knight at Indiana, has expressed deep respect and admiration for his former coach. He credits

Knight with helping him become a better player and leader.

Pat Knight (Texas Tech University): Bob Knight's son, Pat Knight, who also played for and later coached with his father, has shared stories about the challenges and rewards of playing for a demanding coach like Bob Knight. He emphasized the value of the discipline and work ethic instilled by his father.

Jay Edwards (Indiana University): Jay Edwards, who was a standout player under Knight at Indiana, has spoken about the positive impact of Knight's coaching on his career and life, highlighting the coach's influence on his development both as a player and as a person.

Luke Harangody (Texas Tech University): Luke Harangody, who played for Bob Knight at Texas Tech, praised Knight's basketball knowledge and the lessons he learned about the game while playing for him.

Calbert Cheaney (Indiana University): Calbert Cheaney, one of Knight's most successful players at Indiana, has spoken about the discipline and structure provided by Knight, which he believes were key to his development as a player and his success in the NBA.

These testimonials and stories from former players offer a glimpse into the profound impact Bob Knight had on their lives and careers. While Knight's coaching style was often demanding and intense, many of his former players expressed gratitude for the lessons and mentorship they received from their legendary coach.

CHAPTER 10, LESSON LEARNED UNDER KNIGHT'S GUIDANCE

Players who had the opportunity to be coached by Bob Knight often learned valuable life lessons in addition to basketball skills. Here are some of the key lessons that many of his players have cited:

Discipline: Bob Knight was known for instilling discipline in his players. They learned the importance of punctuality, hard work, and adherence to rules and team standards. This discipline extended beyond the court and into their daily lives.

Fundamentals: Knight emphasized mastering the fundamentals of basketball. Players learned the importance of sound passing, shooting, dribbling, and defensive positioning. This focus on fundamentals has served them well both as players and in understanding the basics of the game.

Teamwork: Knight stressed the value of teamwork and unselfish play. Players learned to work together, to trust their teammates, and to put the team's success above personal accomplishments.

Work Ethic: Knight's demanding coaching style instilled a strong work ethic in his players. They realized that success required hard work, commitment, and relentless effort, both in practice and during games.

Accountability: Players under Knight's guidance were held accountable for their actions on and off the court. They learned that their decisions had consequences and that personal responsibility was crucial.

Leadership: Many players had the opportunity to develop leadership skills while playing for Knight. They often had to take on leadership roles within the team, and these experiences helped them become leaders in various aspects of life.

Respect for the Game: Knight instilled a deep respect for the game of basketball and its traditions. Players learned the importance of playing the game with integrity and sportsmanship.

Academic Excellence: Knight emphasized the value of academic success alongside athletic achievement. Players learned to excel in the classroom and understand the importance of education.

Perseverance: Playing for Knight required perseverance in the face of challenges and adversity. Players developed mental toughness and the ability to overcome obstacles.

Mentorship: Many players regarded Knight as a mentor, someone who offered guidance and support not only in their basketball careers but in their personal lives as well.

These lessons went beyond the basketball court, influencing the lives and character of the players who had the privilege of being coached by Bob Knight. While Knight's coaching style was demanding and intense, the impact he had on his players extended far beyond their time as athletes.

CONCLUSION

Bob Knight is a legendary figure in the world of basketball, known for his storied coaching career, distinctive coaching style, and significant impact on the sport. Here are some key points to summarize Bob Knight's legacy:

1. Coaching Legacy: Bob Knight's coaching career spanned several decades and included successful tenures at Indiana University and Texas Tech University. He was celebrated for his coaching achievements, including NCAA championships and numerous tournament appearances.

2. Coaching Philosophy: Knight's coaching philosophy was built on discipline, fundamentals, teamwork, and a strong work ethic. He popularized the "motion offense" and "motion defense" strategies, which have had a lasting impact on coaching at all levels.

3. Player Development: Knight's influence extended to player development. Many of his former players went on to have successful careers in the NBA and other professional leagues, thanks to the skills and values instilled by their coach.

4. Life Lessons: Beyond basketball, Bob Knight taught his players valuable life lessons, such as discipline, accountability, teamwork, leadership, and respect for the game. These lessons had a profound impact on the character and development of his athletes.

5. Broadcasting Career: After retiring from coaching, Knight transitioned to a broadcasting career, where he shared his insights and analysis on college basketball. His contributions to commentary enriched the viewing experience for basketball fans.

6. **Complex Legacy:** Bob Knight's legacy is multifaceted. While he is widely celebrated for his coaching success and contributions to the sport, he was also a polarizing figure due to controversies, confrontational behavior, and off-court incidents.

7. Impact on Players: Many of Knight's former players have spoken about the enduring impact of his coaching and mentorship. They credit him with their development as both players and individuals.

Bob Knight's impact on basketball and his enduring legacy make him one of the most iconic and influential figures in the history of the sport. His contributions to coaching, player development, and the broader basketball community continue to be celebrated and studied by enthusiasts and professionals alike.

Made in United States
Troutdale, OR
11/27/2023

14998510R00053